Repairing the
U.S.-Israel Relationship

COUNCIL on FOREIGN RELATIONS

Council Special Report No. 76
November 2016

Robert D. Blackwill and Philip H. Gordon

Repairing the U.S.-Israel Relationship

The Council on Foreign Relations (CFR) is an independent, nonpartisan membership organization, think tank, and publisher dedicated to being a resource for its members, government officials, business executives, journalists, educators and students, civic and religious leaders, and other interested citizens in order to help them better understand the world and the foreign policy choices facing the United States and other countries. Founded in 1921, CFR carries out its mission by maintaining a diverse membership, with special programs to promote interest and develop expertise in the next generation of foreign policy leaders; convening meetings at its headquarters in New York and in Washington, DC, and other cities where senior government officials, members of Congress, global leaders, and prominent thinkers come together with Council members to discuss and debate major international issues; supporting a Studies Program that fosters independent research, enabling CFR scholars to produce articles, reports, and books and hold roundtables that analyze foreign policy issues and make concrete policy recommendations; publishing *Foreign Affairs*, the preeminent journal on international affairs and U.S. foreign policy; sponsoring Independent Task Forces that produce reports with both findings and policy prescriptions on the most important foreign policy topics; and providing up-to-date information and analysis about world events and American foreign policy on its website, CFR.org.

The Council on Foreign Relations takes no institutional positions on policy issues and has no affiliation with the U.S. government. All views expressed in its publications and on its website are the sole responsibility of the author or authors.

Council Special Reports (CSRs) are concise policy briefs, produced to provide a rapid response to a developing crisis or contribute to the public's understanding of current policy dilemmas. CSRs are written by individual authors—who may be CFR fellows or acknowledged experts from outside the institution—in consultation with an advisory committee, and are intended to take sixty days from inception to publication. The committee serves as a sounding board and provides feedback on a draft report. It usually meets twice— once before a draft is written and once again when there is a draft for review; however, advisory committee members, unlike Task Force members, are not asked to sign off on the report or to otherwise endorse it. Once published, CSRs are posted on www.cfr.org.

For further information about CFR or this Special Report, please write to the Council on Foreign Relations, 58 East 68th Street, New York, NY 10065, or call the Communications office at 212.434.9888. Visit our website, CFR.org.

To submit a letter in response to a Council Special Report for publication on our website, CFR.org, you may send an email to CSReditor@cfr.org. Alternatively, letters may be mailed to us at: Publications Department, Council on Foreign Relations, 58 East 68th Street, New York, NY 10065. Letters should include the writer's name, postal address, and daytime phone number. Letters may be edited for length and clarity, and may be published online. Please do not send attachments. All letters become the property of the Council on Foreign Relations and will not be returned. We regret that, owing to the volume of correspondence, we cannot respond to every letter.

This report is printed on paper that is FSC ® Chain-of-Custody Certified by a printer who is certified by BM TRADA North America Inc.

Contents

Foreword

To say that the U.S.-Israel relationship must be repaired is to say that it is broken. It is—not irretrievably, but seriously. Personalities and policy differences are partly responsible for bringing matters to this point, but there are other, more deep-seated explanations, including demographic changes at work within both Israel and the United States as well as the simple passage of time. The result: two countries that are more different and distant than has been the case for most of Israel's existence.

I anticipate that some reading this Council Special Report will be quick to point out that crises in the U.S.-Israel relationship are hardly new, and that, as in the past, the two sides will find a way to manage their differences. This judgment may be true, but it could just as easily prove to be overly sanguine. More to the point, though, the relationship will not just fix itself. Rather, it will require sustained, high-level attention from both the existing Israeli government and the incoming Trump administration, along with a willingness to take the interests of the other into account. It is precisely such attention and flexibility that have been conspicuously absent in recent years.

This state of affairs and the growing strategic divergence that has emerged serves the interests of neither country. This is especially true given the profound turmoil that characterizes and is all but certain to continue to characterize the Middle East. Indeed, there is good reason to believe threats to regional instability could multiply in coming years, and if they do, both Israel and the United States will face difficult choices about what is to be done—choices that will grow in difficulty and diminish in prospects for success if the two countries are unable to collaborate closely.

The good news is that *Repairing the U.S.-Israel Relationship* was written by Robert D. Blackwill, the Henry A. Kissinger senior fellow for U.S. foreign policy at the Council on Foreign Relations, and Philip H. Gordon, also a senior fellow at the Council. They are respected former practitioners who have spent extensive time at both the State Department and the National Security Council. There is nothing partisan in what they write, even though Robert Blackwill held senior positions in the administration of George W. Bush and Philip Gordon in that of Barack Obama.

The two are not content to simply note problems and discuss their causes and consequences. They also prescribe. What they propose and develop are steps that the new American president should commit to, starting with undertaking and institutionalizing a genuine high-level strategic dialogue with Israel, one that covers the entire region and a host of existing and potential political and military contingencies. They persuasively argue for the two governments developing and implementing a joint strategy to meet the continuing challenges posed by Iran in the nuclear domain and beyond. And they make the case for expanded economic and defense cooperation between the two countries.

Not surprisingly, the matter of Israel's policy toward and relationship with the Palestinians also garners considerable attention from the authors. Here they note the widening gap between many in Israel and the United States over the desirability and feasibility of pursuing a two-state solution to this long-standing conflict. They then go on to suggest a more conditional American approach that would tie elements of U.S. policy to a range of Israeli actions on the ground, including settlement policy and what Israel is prepared to do to improve the daily lives of Palestinians and prospects for the emergence of a viable Palestinian state.

This is an important report. I expect for some it may go too far, for others not far enough. But whatever the reaction, it merits close reading, as it sheds light on a critical set of issues and a critical relationship at a critical time in the history of Israel, the United States, and the Middle East.

Richard N. Haass
President
Council on Foreign Relations
November 2016

Acknowledgments

This Council Special Report benefitted from discussions held during a CFR study group that met monthly in New York from October 2015 to May 2016. The authors are grateful to all the speakers and participants in that group, to several outside reviewers of the draft, and to government officials and experts in Israel and the United States who spoke to us during the course of our research. The analysis and conclusions of the report are the responsibility of the authors alone.

Robert Blackwill
Philip Gordon

Council Special Report

Introduction

The U.S. relationship with Israel is in trouble. The cause of the difficulty is not a mere lack of personal chemistry between Barack Obama and Benjamin Netanyahu, nor can it be reduced to a single policy disagreement, such as the debate over the Iran nuclear deal. Rather, serious differences on a long list of policy issues in the Middle East and significant demographic and political changes on both sides are pushing the two countries apart and making it harder for those who care deeply about the relationship—as we, the authors, do—to maintain it.

A growing number of Israelis—perhaps now a majority—support policies likely to exacerbate differences with the United States and increasingly question their ability to count on Washington, and an increasing number of Americans—including some of Israel's traditional supporters—are concerned about Israel's domestic and foreign policy paths. Without a deliberate and sustained effort by policymakers and opinion leaders in both countries, the relationship will continue to deteriorate, to the detriment of both countries. Various forms of cooperation between the United States and Israel will continue, as they do with many countries in the region, but the shared strategic perspectives, cultural affinity, mutual admiration, and common democratic values that have underpinned the partnership are increasingly at risk. A split between the United States and Israel is an outcome no one who cares about Israel's security or America's values and interests in the Middle East should want.

The sorts of tensions seen during the past few years are, of course, hardly new in the relationship between Washington and Jerusalem; they have existed since Israel's founding during the administration of Harry Truman. Indeed, having served between us in every administration since Richard Nixon, we have seen up close how the two countries have clashed repeatedly, as leaders on both sides fumed about the policies of the other even while stressing their strong instinctive fidelity to

common values and security. But though practically every U.S. administration since Israel's founding in 1948 has had its "crisis" with Israel—
some at least as serious as the Obama administration's dispute over the
Iran nuclear program—the factors that allowed the relationship to bend
but not break are no longer as powerful as they once were. Overlooking
what is new and different, and complacently assuming the relationship
will recover this time as it always has in the past, could prove to be a
dangerous mistake.

Recent trends are especially worrisome because a further split
between the two countries would be more costly than many on either
side want to acknowledge. Israel prides itself on being able to "defend
itself by itself," but the reality is that it continues to rely heavily on the
United States for both military and diplomatic support. The United
States has provided Israel some $100 billion in defense assistance since
the 1979 Camp David peace treaty and regularly expends an enormous
amount of political capital at the United Nations and in a wide range
of other international organizations to shield Israel from criticism or
sanction. Israel can choose to shrug off concerns about growing differences with Washington if it wants, but a decline in support from the
United States would only embolden Israel's enemies and imperil its
legitimacy and security.

Despite the arguments of some of Israel's critics, the United States
profits substantially from the relationship as well. Israel is the United
States' closest strategic partner in the world's most unstable region and
shares valuable intelligence with Washington on terrorism, nonprolif-
eration, and regional politics. The United States also derives important
military benefits from the partnership, in areas such as military technology, intelligence, joint training and exercises, and cybersecurity.[1] And,
despite its relatively small population, Israel is the largest regional inves-
tor in the United States, the third largest destination for U.S. exports in
the Middle East, an important research and development partner for
the U.S. high-tech sector, and a source of innovative ideas on confront-
ing twenty-first-century challenges such as renewable energy and water
and food security.[2]

Given the real structural challenges facing the relationship, there
is no quick fix for the divisions that have emerged. But repairing and
preserving the relationship is possible if the two governments and concerned citizens in both countries appreciate how much is at stake. This
Council Special Report examines the ways in which U.S. and Israeli

strategic perspectives have diverged in recent years, explores how social, generational, and demographic changes in both countries challenge the relationship, and concludes with six core policy proposals to repair, redefine, and invigorate the partnership:

- Seek to reframe the relationship at a summit in early 2017 at Camp David focused on developing a new strategic vision for a changing Middle East, committing the United States to remain engaged in the region, seriously addressing the Palestinian problem, and institutionalizing an intensive bilateral strategic dialogue.

- Enhance Israel's sense of security and confidence in the United States by committing to expanded missile defense, anti-tunnel, and cyber-security cooperation under the terms of the September 2016 long-term defense assistance Memorandum of Understanding (MOU).

- Move beyond the debate about the merits of the Iran nuclear agreement and work together to implement and rigorously enforce it, with a commitment to imposing penalties on Iran for noncompliance and a joint plan for preventing Iran from developing nuclear weapons after the deal's main restrictions expire.

- Develop detailed common understandings about how to more effectively contain Iranian hegemonic regional designs and take action designed to do so.

- Agree on a set of specific, meaningful measures that Israel will take unilaterally to improve Palestinian daily life and preserve prospects for a two-state solution, linking continued U.S. willingness to refrain from or oppose international action on Israeli settlements or the peace process to Israel's implementation of such positive, concrete steps.

- Expand economic cooperation focused on bilateral trade, investment, energy, innovation, and Israel's integration into the region.

The Threat of Strategic Divergence

The most basic risk to the U.S.-Israel relationship is a growing divergence over how to handle the most serious dangers to Israel's security—or even existence. For decades, "ensuring Israel's security" meant making sure Israel had the military power and intelligence capacities to defend against invading Arab armies, individually or collectively, and at that task the two countries succeeded spectacularly. As Amos Yadlin, the former head of military intelligence for the Israeli Defense Forces, recently noted, "The conventional threat posed by the regular armies of the neighboring countries has all but vanished."[3]

Nonetheless, U.S. conventional military support for Israel has not only continued strongly but also increased in recent years. During the Obama administration alone, the United States provided Israel nearly $24 billion in defense assistance, including more than $1.2 billion for missile defense systems such as Iron Dome, which proved so effective in the 2014 Gaza War.[4] The United States is selling Israel its advanced F-35 Joint Strike Fighters (making Israel the only country in the region to receive them) and has approved an unprecedented release of military capabilities, including V-22 Osprey aircraft (also a first), KC-135 tankers, AESA (active electronically scanned array) radars for Israel's F-15 and F-16 fighters, and anti-radiation missiles. Prime Minister Netanyahu and former Israeli Defense Minister Moshe Ya'alon have repeatedly expressed great satisfaction with recent U.S.-Israel security collaboration, which longtime senior U.S. official Dennis Ross—who helped design that collaboration in the Ronald Reagan administration—has confirmed goes "beyond what any previous administration has put in place."[5] The next administration will almost certainly be similarly committed to sustaining Israel's qualitative military edge over its adversaries in the region.

The problem is that, unlike in past decades, today's main security challenge is not just deterring an invasion of Arab armies, a specific and well-defined mission on which the United States and Israel were easily able to unite. Instead, the primary threats Israel faces today come from elsewhere: an expansionist, potentially nuclear-armed Iran; spreading disorder and the rise of terrorist nonstate regional actors armed with missiles and supported by outside powers; and a growing and increasingly discontented Arab population within and on Israel's borders. U.S. and Israeli perspectives on how to deal with all these critical issues are currently far apart and may be structurally diverging.

The most glaring recent difference has, of course, been the bitter bilateral dispute over the Iran nuclear program. Washington and Jerusalem concur strongly on the objective—preventing Iran from acquiring a nuclear weapon—but disagree equally strongly on how to achieve that goal. For Obama, it has meant negotiating the best diplomatic agreement he considered possible, one that constrained Iran's nuclear program (including uranium enrichment, plutonium production, research and development of centrifuges, and work to turn nuclear material into weapons) for a significant amount of time and put an expanded monitoring and verification regime permanently in place. Obama has deemed this a far preferable alternative to merely maintaining sanctions and pressure as the Iranian program continued to expand or, alternatively, setting the nuclear program back temporarily with military force and all its inevitable unintended consequences. For Netanyahu, on the other hand, preventing a nuclear-armed Iran means doing everything he can to constrain and avoid legitimizing Iran's uranium enrichment program which, he fears, could ultimately pave the way to an Iranian nuclear weapon, a concern shared by the United States' Arab allies.

The result of these differences was the ugly, unprecedented spectacle of an Israeli prime minister provocatively speaking to a joint session of Congress against a U.S. president's foreign policy priority—a move opposed by even some of Israel's strongest supporters in the United States. As journalist Jeffrey Goldberg put it, the speech put even "American Jewish supporters of Israel in a messy, uncomfortable spot," one "in which they have to choose between their president and the leader of a Jewish state whose behavior is making them queasy."[6]

Netanyahu's willingness to risk this clash with Israel's most powerful ally underscored the depth of the gap between the two governments. Netanyahu chose to publicly undercut the U.S. president because he was convinced that Israel's survival was at stake. His close advisor, Ambassador to the United States Ron Dermer, later said the speech was the "highlight of his tenure" in Washington and that for Netanyahu speaking out on the issue was so important that it was "worth the price" of strained ties with Obama.[7] And though many Israelis were uncomfortable with the clash with the United States and the timing of a speech so close to Israeli elections, on the substance of the deal they strongly agreed with their prime minister. Opinion polls consistently showed that some three-quarters of Israelis thought the nuclear deal posed a threat to Israel, and nearly half believed that Israel should conduct an attack on Iran to prevent it from obtaining a nuclear weapon.[8]

The Obama administration also strongly opposes a nuclear-armed Iran, of course. But wary of the consequences of a military intervention to set the program back, contending with ongoing wars in Iraq, Afghanistan, and Syria, and faced with poor policy alternatives, it also remains strongly averse to getting involved in another Middle East conflict so long as a diplomatic solution seems possible. This was also the case during the George W. Bush administration, which remained focused on diplomacy even as Iran mastered the nuclear fuel cycle and developed its enrichment program.

Another difference between the two countries is that vast military capabilities give the United States much more flexibility when it comes to coping with the Iranian threat; Washington has the relative luxury of waiting to see whether and how the danger develops. Conversely, as Tehran's nuclear capability has advanced, Jerusalem has seen the window for its own military option narrow, producing understandable anxieties across Israel's body politic. Given its diverse interests in the region, the United States also inevitably places a higher relative priority on other regional goals that would suffer from an all-out confrontation with Iran—such as promoting stability in Iraq and defeating the self-declared Islamic State. Israelis, on the other hand, necessarily focus more on the existential threat of a nuclear Iran, which Dermer and other Israelis argue is "a thousand times more dangerous than ISIS."[9] Under these circumstances, it is not surprising that though both the United States and Israel are determined in principle to prevent a nuclear Iran, they differ on how to go about doing so. The nuclear agreement has bought time, but this fundamental difference in approach will persist.

In addition to deep disagreements over Iran's nuclear threat, Washington and Jerusalem differ in their policy regarding Iran more broadly.[10] Israelis fear that behind the nuclear deal is a naive U.S. attempt at a larger rapprochement with an enemy that rejects Israel's right to exist,

supports terrorist groups that attack it, and has aspirations of hege-
mony in the region. The expansion of an Iranian corridor of influence
from Tehran to the Mediterranean has given Iran unprecedented power
projection capabilities in the area. Iranian proxies, including Lebanese
Hezbollah—which has more than a hundred thousand missiles and
rockets pointed at Israel—today have extensive freedom of movement
from Tehran right up to Israel's border. In every country where Iran's
power is expanding, Israelis see insufficient resistance from Washington, leading them to conclude that the Obama administration is so
invested in the success of the nuclear deal and so averse to conflict in the
region that it is willing to acquiesce to Tehran's hegemonic designs. The
assumption that the Obama administration is prioritizing the nuclear
deal at the expense of defending against Tehran's imperial ambitions is
one that Israel again shares with the United States' Arab allies.

Jerusalem also takes issue with the Obama administration's approach
toward Egypt. Israeli leaders and strategists believe it is counterproduc-
tive, especially at a time of chaos in the Middle East, for the United States
to press Arab governments over their internal political arrangements
and human rights practices. The Obama administration suspended
deliveries of major weapons systems to Egypt after the military crack-
down in the summer of 2013 and has denied Egyptian President Abdel
Fatah al-Sisi the Oval Office meeting Egyptian presidents had come to
expect, even as Cairo has intensified its strategic partnership with Israel
and maintains arguably the most pro-Israel policies in Egypt's history.
With the two greatest threats to Israel—Iran and international terrorism—both increasing, Jerusalem asserts that Washington should prioritize stability in Egypt over democracy and human rights and presses
the United States to maintain its military assistance.[11] Even as the
Obama administration has proceeded to restore most of that assistance
and tone down its critiques of the Sisi regime, Israelis have complained
that U.S. normalization of the relationship has not gone far enough and
have encouraged even closer strategic cooperation with Cairo. Israel's
primary interest is in maintaining its peace treaty and counterterrorism
cooperation with Egypt, and Israelis argue that U.S. criticism of Arab
governments' internal affairs is more effective when voiced privately,
given that public rebukes are ineffective and only antagonize U.S. partners in the Arab world.

The United States and Israel have also been misaligned regarding
Syria, where once again Israel prioritizes the quest for stability and

deterrence over efforts to promote democracy or regime change.[12] Whereas early on in the Syrian conflict Washington announced a policy of getting rid of Assad, a brutal dictator whose autocratic rule breeds radicalization and terrorism, Jerusalem has remained comparatively nostalgic for the "devil it knew"—an Assad regime that had maintained relative stability for decades. Although the Obama administration has gradually downgraded the priority of promoting regime change in Syria, its continued support for opposition elements in the name of that goal have stoked Israeli fears of rising Islamist extremism and post-Assad chaos in Syria. Israel also has an interest in countering Iranian influence in Syria, of course, particularly Iran's proxy Hezbollah. But Jerusalem is convinced that an all-out military campaign to oust Assad will only empower another enemy—Islamist extremists—and prefers to focus on containment of both threats and to prioritize threats to Israel's territory. Since Russia began attacking targets in Syria in September 2015, Prime Minister Netanyahu has not criticized the expanded Russian military presence or its strikes on U.S.-backed rebel groups on behalf of Assad. Instead, he has met with President Vladimir Putin four times since September 2015 in an effort to coordinate Israeli-Russian policy toward Syria; their focus has been on preventing Hezbollah's acquisition of advanced missiles, not on removing Assad.[13] Jerusalem is thus pursuing closer cooperation with Moscow both in Syria and in general, and many Americans worry about the corrosive strategic consequences of Russia's reentry into the Middle East.

Finally, but perhaps most important, is the growing U.S.-Israel gap over the Palestinian issue. For all the obvious obstacles to achieving a two-state solution, most Americans (inside and outside government, and including a majority of American Jews) still see no realistic alternatives to it. They believe that Israeli policy, especially when it comes to settlements on the West Bank, should be designed to keep prospects for that eventual outcome alive. They believe that any alternative to a two-state solution would mean a necessarily undemocratic Israel governing millions of Palestinians in a way that would undermine the common values on which the U.S.-Israel relationship has been built. This line of thinking has underpinned the Obama administration's approach to the issue (just as it had that of previous administrations), including its efforts to get Israel to curb settlement building it considered an obstacle to peace and to broker comprehensive bilateral negotiations between the two sides.

Many Israelis, on the other hand, appear to be giving up on the two-state solution. After years of failed negotiating efforts, growing questions about any Palestinian leader's willingness or ability to conclude a deal, and the results of Israel's unilateral withdrawal from Gaza (Hamas control of the territory and ongoing terrorist attacks with rockets and through tunnels), an increasing number of Israelis are reaching the conclusion that there will never be a Palestinian state they can live with. According to polls conducted by Hebrew University, Israeli support for a two-state solution has fallen from a recent peak of 79 percent in 2008 to just 51 percent in 2015.[14] Some 88 percent of Israelis now do not believe the Palestinians are making a sincere effort for peace, and more than three-quarters of Israeli Jews do not believe that negotiations with the Palestinians will lead to peace.[15] For the first time in twenty years, a majority of the Israeli cabinet is made up of ministers who officially oppose the creation of a Palestinian state.

The U.S.-Israel divergence on the Palestinian issue is particularly severe when it comes to the question of settlements. Israeli governments of both left and right have long tolerated or supported settlement growth, and even those Israeli leaders personally uncommitted to the settlement project have not been willing to pay the political price of significantly curbing its growth. The Israeli settlement population in the West Bank has risen from a few tens of thousands in the 1970s, to around 120,000 at the time of the 1993 Oslo Accords, to at least 370,000 (including at least 85,000 in settlements deep in the West Bank, beyond the main settlement blocs) today. The Israeli population in disputed East Jerusalem has during the same period risen to more than 200,000. Since Netanyahu came back to power in 2009, the West Bank settler population has grown by some 80,000 (including 16,000 deep in the West Bank), with construction begun on 9,000 new settlement units on the West Bank and 3,000 more in East Jerusalem.[16] Netanyahu has permitted the construction of new settlement units at about the same rate as his immediate predecessors, but the cumulative effect of expansion, the rising natural growth of the settlement population, the location of the settlements (in some cases specifically chosen to limit territorial contiguity for Palestinians), and the absence of serious peace talks has made the issue increasingly problematic.[17] In recent years, Israel also has been accelerating the process of retroactively "legalizing" outposts across the West Bank but only rarely dismantling them—thus further extending its footprint on the West Bank.[18] As all this activity goes on,

Israel is preventing nearly all Palestinian development or construction for housing, industrial zones, tourism, or infrastructure in the West Bank and East Jerusalem and demolishing hundreds of Palestinian structures in both areas.[19]

Netanyahu downplays the importance of settlement building in the Israeli-Palestinian conflict and often insists that it is unfair to equate Palestinian terrorism and incitement to "a few more apartments near the municipality of Ma'ale Adumim or a few neighborhoods in Jerusalem."[20] He has said he does not accept "the idea that we must uproot and ethnically cleanse the Jews who live in Judea and Samaria" and insists that settlement construction is "not what is preventing an agreement."[21] He argues that because Arabs fought Israel's existence for decades before the first settlements were established after 1967, they are clearly "not the core of the problem."[22] In September 2016, Netanyahu released a controversial video statement not only denying that Israeli settlements are an obstacle to peace but suggesting that opposing them amounts to "ethnic cleansing" of Jews.[23]

Many Israelis also seem to believe that Israel's current strategic situation is robust enough that it need not be responsive to the Obama administration's—or the world's—distress over Israel's settlement activity. They note support for Israel remains strong in the U.S. Congress, there is no conventional military threat to Israel, Israel's relations with the Arab monarchies and Egypt have never been better, terrorism against Israel is limited, and the Palestinian movement is divided and ineffective. Israelis tend to dismiss the long-term costs and consequences of their settlement policies, and reject any linkage to their ability to deal with regional challenges that could emerge suddenly—from an Iranian nuclear breakout to an Islamist takeover in Amman, Riyadh, or Cairo, or to a third intifada. In contrast to American warnings that the status quo is unsustainable, many Israelis on both sides of the political spectrum now believe that the Israeli consensus on the issue is that "the occupation as it is now can last forever, and it is better than any alternative."[24]

In contrast, successive U.S. administrations have long felt that Israeli settlements undermine both Israeli and U.S. national interests. First, they are a major and growing obstacle to the territorial compromises that would be necessary to achieve a two-state solution, which has been the policy goal of the United States for more than twenty years; most interested Americans do not believe Israel can remain a secure, Jewish, and democratic state if it seeks to govern lands where millions of disenfranchised Palestinians live. Second, the enduring resonance of the conflict in the Muslim world and widespread perceptions of injustice toward Palestinians makes settlement activity a driver of Islamist radicalization. Israeli occupation of the West Bank is far from the dominant factor in radicalization today in the region at large, but because settlement construction undermines a sense of justice and dignity for Palestinians and the possibility of a peaceful end to the conflict, it remains an issue for radicals to use in their narrative, weakening U.S. efforts to counter violent extremism. Third, the issue of settlements is easily used by the boycott, divestment, and sanctions (BDS) movement to paint Israel in a negative light, which divides Americans and undermines support for Israel in the United States. As long as the United States is seen as the primary—or perhaps sole—defender of Israel while Israeli settlement activities violate international law in most of the world's eyes, U.S. political capital will dwindle and American credibility will suffer in the region and abroad.

These divergent perspectives over the Palestinian issue have led to serious strains in the bilateral relationship. In February 2014, in the midst of Secretary of State John Kerry's pursuit of an agreed framework for Israeli-Palestinian peace, Defense Minister Ya'alon called the U.S. security plan for the West Bank "not worth the paper it is written on." He complained that Kerry was pursuing negotiations out of "misplaced obsession and messianic fervor" and should just "leave us in peace."[25] Apparently appealing to Israelis who shared that view, in the run-up to the March 2015 Israeli elections, Netanyahu boasted about how his support for strategically placed settlements would make the formation of a Palestinian state more difficult and pledged that no Palestinian state would be established while he was prime minister.[26]

In response, the Obama administration announced that it was reassessing its approach, and White House Chief of Staff Denis McDonough said Netanyahu's remarks "call into question his commitment to a two-state solution."[27] Even after the collapse of talks, Kerry continued to insist that a two-state solution was the only strategically sensible option and that "unless significant efforts are made to change the dynamic—and I mean significant—it will only bring more violence, more heartbreak, and more despair."[28] In April 2016, Vice President Joe Biden—like Kerry, a long-standing friend of Israel—said he firmly believed that "the actions that Israel's government has taken over the past several years—the steady and systematic expansion of settlements, the legalization of outposts, land seizures" were "moving us and more importantly they're moving Israel in the wrong direction." He added that it was the U.S. obligation to "push . . . as hard as we can" toward a two-state solution despite "our sometimes overwhelming frustration with the Israeli government."[29] In late 2016, with little to show for eight years of efforts to advance Middle East peace, the Obama administration was reported to be considering putting forward parameters—or even a potential UN Security Council resolution—for a future peace agreement.[30] Netanyahu has made clear how strongly he would oppose such efforts.[31]

Again, this is hardly the first time the United States and Israel have disagreed about the Palestinians, settlements, or the right approach to peace. But as 2016 comes to an end, hopes for a solution, or even for a common U.S.-Israeli approach, seem lower than ever. A look at domestic trends within each country suggests that, without real effort on both sides, the gaps are only going to get worse.

Societies Growing Apart

Looking broadly at public attitudes in Israel and the United States, along with the repeated pledges of political leaders in both countries of devotion to the relationship, there would seem to be little cause for concern about its future. Overall U.S. support for Israel remains strong, and majorities in both countries continue to view the other country favorably. In 2015, for example, even in the midst of the dispute over Iran, 81 percent of Israelis said they had a positive view of the United States, and 79 percent of Americans viewed Israel as either an ally or a country friendly to the United States.[32] Some 62 percent of Americans, moreover, said their sympathies were more with the Israelis than with the Palestinians (23 percent), and 45 percent of Americans saw Israel as such an important ally that the United States should support it "even if our interests diverge."[33] Both major party candidates for the U.S. presidency repeatedly stressed their unshakeable support for Israel, a position that a large majority in Congress shares.

That said, within the overall picture of continued mutual support, some trends are troubling. On the Israeli side, they involve a population that is becoming more religious, nationalistic, and conservative, exacerbating differences with Washington on issues ranging from the state of liberalism and democracy in Israel to policy toward the Palestinians and Iran. Meanwhile, in the United States, the issues include a youth population less sympathetic to Israel than their older counterparts, demographic trends likely to give more political power to groups less traditionally supportive of Israel, an increasingly divided U.S. Jewish community, and—perhaps most troublingly—a growing and unprecedented partisan gap over Israel. None of these trends will necessarily lead to divorce between the United States and Israel, but to ignore their existence would be irresponsible.

Israel has unquestionably become more conservative, nationalistic, and illiberal in recent years, in part because of the makeup of its population. One important factor driving this trend is the rapid growth of Israel's ultra-Orthodox population. Haredi or ultra-Orthodox Jews already account for some 11 percent of the Israeli population; given their much higher birthrate than the rest of the population, that percentage is expected to rise to around 18 percent by 2030. This more conservative and religious Israel not only distances it from the liberal and democratic values of the United States but also further undermines the prospects for a two-state solution. According to a 2016 Pew survey, 99 percent of Orthodox settlers believe that "God gave Judea and Samaria to the Jewish people" and 65 percent believe that "Arabs should be expelled or transferred" from the West Bank.[34]

The growth—and growing political influence—of the Israeli settler population is another important factor. Influential even when their numbers were smaller, Israelis living on the West Bank and in East Jerusalem (nearly six hundred thousand today) inevitably affect the composition of Israeli governments and the policies they pursue. Given that the population growth rate in settlements is more than two and a half times that of the Jewish-Israeli national average, the settler population is now growing autonomously faster than immigration: in 2013, 75 percent of settlement population growth was from Jews who were born there, and only 25 percent was from relocation and immigration.[35] Because the settler population is generally more conservative and religious than the rest of the Israeli population and by definition committed to an aspect of Israeli policy that U.S. administrations have defined as an obstacle to peace, its continued growth—even aside from the issue of new settlement construction—will only add to growing bilateral differences with the United States.

These demographic changes, along with the growing security concerns of the wider Israeli population, have led to the formation of the most right-wing coalition in Israel's history. In the 2015 elections, right-wing parties, including the ultra-Orthodox, took 67 of the Knesset's 120 seats, with the Left down to 53 seats. Netanyahu formed a government with a one-seat majority, including the ultra-Orthodox parties. In May 2016, that government moved even further to the right with the inclusion of former Foreign Minister Avigdor Lieberman's right-wing, nationalist Yisrael Beiteinu party. The move expanded Netanyahu's narrow majority, but the price was to give the Defense Ministry to Lieberman, an immigrant from Russia who lives on a settlement in the West Bank and has a history of ultranationalist positions and controversial statements about Palestinians. When asked at a December 2015 conference in Washington for his reaction to concerns that criticism of Israel was rising not just among its opponents but also among traditional supporters and American Jews, Lieberman responded, "To speak frankly, I don't care."[36]

The new government's orientation includes not only skepticism about a two-state solution and vigorous support for settlement expansion, but also potentially illiberal measures within Israel. Recent reflections of this include draft legislation to define Israel as "the nation-state of the Jewish people" in ways that could discriminate against Arab and other non-Jewish citizens of Israel; another bill that would single out Israeli nongovernmental organizations that receive significant foreign government financing, which critics claimed would mostly ostracize groups that monitor Israeli human rights practices; provisions to ban or deport supporters of BDS from Israel; a new law that would allow a three-fourths majority in the Knesset to expel another member from the Knesset; and the use of punitive home demolitions of relatives of Palestinian (but not Jewish) terrorists—practices that have been criticized by the United States and others around the world. All these measures are consistent with survey data that shows the Israeli population's growing prioritization of Israel's Jewish identity over its democratic identity—a tendency particularly pronounced among Israeli youth.[37]

Even after a new administration takes office in Washington, it seems fair to conclude that on a range of both domestic and foreign policy issues, major policy differences with the United States will remain.

This is all the more true because the United States is also changing in ways that could make cooperation more difficult. The first trend worth considering is that younger Americans—those born after 1980—are markedly less supportive of Israel than previous generations. These Americans came to political age not when Israel was the plucky little democracy standing up to hostile Arabs who refused to compromise, but instead more recently, when Israel has been the stronger regional power. In part as a result, they have distinctly different views of Israel than older segments of population. As scholars Dana Allin and Steven Simon argue in a recent book surveying American attitudes toward Israel since its foundation, "The commitment of a postwar generation to the ideals of Zionism is fading as that generation moves toward old age."[38]

Some recent surveys substantiate that narrative: although Americans of all age groups sympathize more with Israelis than with Palestinians, the gap is by far the smallest (16 points) among those under age thirty-six. It is 47 points for those between fifty-two and seventy and 50 points for those older than seventy. This trend cannot be attributed to a perspective expected to change as this younger group ages, given that in the past a similar age gap did not exist—indeed, ten years ago the younger cohort actually showed more relative sympathy to Israelis than older Americans did.[39] Among young Democrats the contrast is even more striking: half of Democrats under thirty (in contrast to all other demographic groups) support punishing Israel with sanctions over settlements, and among those who believe the United States should "lean toward" one side or the other in the conflict, a slight majority of Democrats under thirty say the tilt should be toward the Palestinians.[40] As Dennis Ross points out, during the 2014 Gaza War, among eighteen- to twenty-nine-year-olds, the U.S. split was nearly even on who was to blame between Israel and Hamas, and even Jewish Americans in that age cohort "are much more prone to question Israeli policies toward the Palestinians."[41] A 2013 Pew survey also showed that a quarter of American Jews between eighteen and twenty-nine said that the United States supports Israel too much, versus only 5 percent of American Jews over fifty.[42]

These trends are reflected in movements at numerous college campuses, where support among students for BDS is growing.[43] They may also explain why Vermont Senator Bernie Sanders, whose predominant support is among youth, put an unusual emphasis on justice for Palestinians in his presidential campaign. In a primary debate in Brooklyn five days before the New York primary, Sanders broke with political convention to complain about his opponent's lack of focus on the Palestinians, arguing that "there will never be peace in that region unless the United States plays an even-handed role."[44] Sanders later went on to appoint two long-standing critics of Israel—James Zogby and Cornel West— to the committee assigned to write the Democratic Party's platform, where they pushed strongly for a recognition of the Israeli "occupation" of the West Bank. Sanders's statement to the committee stressed that "lasting peace in the region will not occur without fair and respectful treatment of the Palestinian people."[45] As this group of Americans ages and moves into positions of power, it will have an effect on the political basis of Israel's support in the United States.

Beyond age groups, the changing ethnic makeup of the American population is also politically relevant in ways unlikely to be favorable to support for Israel. U.S. approval of Israel has, of course, always been widespread across multiple ethnic and religious groups. But it is stronger among some groups (Jewish Americans and Evangelicals) than others (including Hispanic, Asian, and African Americans). For example, Hispanic Americans want the United States to remain neutral in the Israeli-Palestinian conflict (as opposed to tilting toward Israel) in significantly higher proportions than the rest of the population. Among those who would like the United States to take a side, fewer want to tilt toward Israel; 44 percent support sanctions on Israel over settlements.[46] African Americans also favor neutrality in the conflict, 80 percent saying that the United States should lean toward neither side; among various ethnicities, African Americans have the highest proportion (78 percent) of those who favor Israel's democracy—including rights for Palestinians—over its Jewish identity.[47] Although the intensity of these feelings is doubtless less powerful than among ethnic groups that prioritize the issue, the size and political strength of these groups is growing considerably. Whereas Hispanic, Asian, and African Americans made up 21 percent of the electorate in 2000, in 2016 that proportion is estimated to be 28 percent—a 7 point rise in just sixteen years.[48] Looking at the population as a whole (not just those of voting age), those groups made up around 20 percent of the population in 1980, a proportion projected to increase to 38 percent by 2020 and to 41 percent by 2030.[49]

Even within the American Jewish community—once strongly united behind support for the Jewish state—attitudes are changing. To be sure, the vast majorities of American Jews still feel a special bond with Israel, and the largest pro-Israel lobbying groups, such as the American Israel Public Affairs Committee (AIPAC), show unstinting support for the policies of the current Israeli government and wield considerable influence in Congress. But the American Jewish community is increasingly divided, and support for Israel no longer translates automatically into support for Israeli government policy. The growth of alternative pro-Israel groups such as J Street and Americans for Peace Now, though they are still much smaller than AIPAC, reflects an increasing diversity of opinion, and these groups are having a growing impact on the debate. According to scholar Dov Waxman, whose new book *Trouble in the Tribe* examines the evolution of American Jewish attitudes toward Israel, "A growing number of American Jews, even a majority, are dissatisfied with Israel's treatment of the Palestinians and deeply worried about Israel's ability to remain a Jewish and democratic state if it continues to effectively rule over Palestinians in the West Bank and East

Jerusalem." Waxman notes that these American Jews worry about "the frightening prospect of Israel becoming increasingly illiberal, and, increasingly isolated in the international community" and warns that "as this happens, many liberal American Jews, especially younger ones, will turn away from Israel in despair, or even disgust."[50]

A final, relevant trend is the growing partisan gap on the Israel issue within the United States. For example, in 2015, 76 percent of Republicans said a candidate's position on Israel was "deeply important" to them, compared to 49 percent of Democrats. And nearly half of Democrats, but only 25 percent of Republicans, thought Israel had too much influence on U.S. policy.[51] In contrast to twenty years ago, when Democrats showed a greater tendency than Republicans to sympathize more with Israelis than Palestinians, today 79 percent of Republicans sympathize more with Israelis, compared with 56 percent of independents and 53 percent of Democrats.[52]

Not surprisingly, these trends are reflected in Republican and Democratic attitudes toward important policy issues. Although nearly half of Republicans think the United States should vote against a UN Security Council resolution endorsing a Palestinian state (or even use its veto to prevent such an endorsement), only 15 percent of Democrats would favor doing so.[53] And whereas 49 percent of Democrats think the United States should respond to continued settlement construction with sanctions, only 26 percent of Republicans support that approach.[54]

The 2016 Republican and Democratic Party platforms reflected this divergence. Whereas in previous election years the two parties' positions on Israel were virtually identical, this year's Republican platform dropped any reference to support for a two-state solution and took hard-line positions that asserted unconstrained Israeli rights not only in recognized Israel but also throughout the West Bank and in all of Jerusalem. It asserted that "support for Israel is an expression of Americanism, and it is the responsibility of our government to advance policies that reflect Americans' strong desire for a relationship with no daylight between America and Israel."[55] The Democratic platform also expressed strong support for Israel, of course, but included traditional support for peace negotiations directly between the parties and recognition that "Palestinians should be free to govern themselves in their own viable state, in peace and dignity." Notably, a proposal that the platform include a call for the "end of occupation and illegal settlements" was only narrowly defeated, ninety-five to seventy-three.[56]

Support for the Iran nuclear deal also predictably broke down along almost exclusively partisan lines. More than 90 percent of congressional Democrats supported the deal, and 100 percent of congressional Republicans shared Israel's opposition to it. Among public opinion, the breakdown was the same: conservative Republicans opposed the deal 82 to 7 percent and moderate/liberal Republicans 58 to 29 percent; conservative/moderate Democrats supported it 48 to 33 percent and liberal Democrats 74 to 14 percent.[57] None of the 2016 Republican candidates for president supported the nuclear deal (with several saying they would "tear it up" on the first day of their presidency), whereas all the Democrats said they would maintain it.

A Practical Agenda for Bridging the Gaps

Middle Easterners, including Israelis, like to remind their American friends that they measure history in decades, centuries, and millennia—not in months and years. Israelis certainly made that point often during debates about the Iran nuclear deal, whose decade-long restrictions on Iran's enrichment capability Netanyahu called "the blink of an eye in the life of a nation," and Israel's enemies often make it about Israel's very existence.[58] But the same point, in fact, could be made about the U.S.-Israel alliance itself, which has only really been around for about fifty years—still a blink of an eye in Middle East terms. Complacently assuming its permanence simply because it has always survived crises before would be shortsighted and damaging to both sides.

Leaders in Jerusalem and Washington can do little to prevent some of the long-term structural trends discussed here. They can, though, do much to rebuild confidence and trust, avoid unnecessary disputes, demonstrate mutual commitment, pursue common national interests together, and listen to the other side more carefully and more sympathetically—all of which will help mitigate those trends. The choices they make will reflect not just how each side sees its national interests—which may in some cases legitimately differ—but also how much they value the bilateral relationship and how willing they are to invest in it. No magic formula exists for improving a relationship that will inevitably have its strains (as it always has), but leaders in Washington and Jerusalem could implement six policy prescriptions after January 2017 to put the relationship on a better track. Failure to do so is likely to prove costly over time.

REFRAME THE RELATIONSHIP

Eight years of bitter disputes over Iran, Palestinians, settlements, the region, and democracy in Israel—aggravated by poor personal relations

between the leaders—have taken their toll on the bilateral relationship. To try to put some of this baggage aside, President-Elect Donald
Trump should invite the Israeli prime minister to Camp David within
a few months of the inauguration for extended talks to frankly and privately discuss agreements and differences and look for opportunities
to work together. With the Middle East in turmoil, and Israeli and U.S.
perspectives on critical challenges diverging, such a sustained exchange
would be an important opportunity for the two leaders to lay out their
perspectives, listen carefully, and frankly address the differences they
have. Based on advance coordination that could be undertaken from
the start of the transition period in Washington, they could seek agreement on a positive agenda that could include the proposals that follow.
The goal would be to develop a new, shared vision for the region that
would include not only renewed U.S. commitments to Israel's security,
an enhanced commitment to jointly meet the challenges posed by Iran,
and U.S. support for Israel's diplomatic alignment with its Arab neigh-
bors, but also an Israeli commitment to address U.S. concerns about the
lack of progress on peace with the Palestinians and the corrosiveness of
Israel's settlement practices on the West Bank.

More specifically, the new administration should stress that the
United States is in the Middle East to stay. This means that it will use its
formidable power and influence there in all dimensions; more directly
confront and defeat Iran's hegemonic designs in the region (Syria, Lebanon, Yemen, the Gulf states); increase resources to defeat the Islamic
State in Iraq, Syria, and Libya; work trilaterally with Israel and Egypt
on regional security; reassure the Arab monarchies and Egypt that
their internal stability is of paramount importance to the United States;
increase U.S. economic and security assistance to Jordan; and weaken
burgeoning Russian influence across the area.

To these ends, the two leaders should announce in that first meeting the institutionalization of a regular strategic channel between the
two countries' national security teams to address changing trends in the
Middle East and what the United States and Israel can do together to
deal with them. Such a channel—known as the U.S.-Israel Consultative
Group—functioned effectively at times during the Obama administration, particularly from 2010 to 2013 under national security advisors
Thomas Donilon in the United States and Yaakov Amidror in Israel, but
it has lost momentum and no meetings have been held for almost two
years. As retired Israeli General Michael Herzog has suggested, such a

channel should include a specific working group on Iran.[59] As previous U.S.-Israel crises have demonstrated, dialogue itself cannot overcome differences when perceptions of national interests genuinely diverge, but early, honest, and transparent communication can help prevent unnecessary resentment and identify ways to manage differences.

EXTEND AND EXPAND DEFENSE COOPERATION

Even in the context of a diminishing threat from conventional regional armies, it remains critical that Israel maintain its qualitative military edge over any combination of potential adversaries. It was therefore encouraging that in September 2016—despite their differences on other issues—Obama and Netanyahu agreed on a new, long-term defense assistance agreement to replace the 2007 Memorandum of Understanding that expires in 2018. According to the new MOU, the United States will provide Israel with $3.3 billion per year in annual foreign military financing for the next ten years, plus an additional $500 million per year that will be devoted to missile defense. The agreement will phase out a special provision that allowed Israel to spend part of the money on its own domestic defense industry, but it will continue to give Israel the flexibility to borrow against future funding (not available to other U.S. defense aid recipients) and to deposit annual assistance in Israel at the start of each fiscal year and keep the interest. It also includes funding for missile defense in the MOU itself (rather than looking to Congress to add it in on an annual basis) and allows for increased assistance in case of an emergency if both governments agree.[60]

Trump and the Israeli prime minister should make clear in their first meeting their commitment to the terms of this MOU. Doing so would demonstrate resolute, long-term U.S. support for Israel's security, sending a critical signal to the citizens of both countries about how committed the leaders are to Israel's security and the U.S.-Israel partnership. Even more important, it would send a signal to Israel's adversaries that whatever differences between Washington and Jerusalem, and even when there is a change of administration in Washington, the U.S. commitment to Israel's security is enduring and absolute.

The inclusion of guaranteed missile defense funding in the MOU is an important step because of the growing threat Israel faces from the missiles, rockets, and mortars held by Hezbollah and Hamas that can target Israeli cities including Jerusalem and Tel Aviv.[61] A second priority for new funding should be joint research on anti-tunneling technology. Addressing Israel's critical vulnerability in this area by assisting in the development of an "underground Iron Dome" would yield beneficial technologies for both countries and help Israel avoid the sort of attacks and kidnappings of civilians or soldiers that are not only tragic but can be used for blackmail. Within the context of the MOU, the United States should provide the $40 million per year requested in the December 2015 omnibus spending bill for anti-tunnel technology development and commit to funding research on and deployment of this technology for as long as necessary. Finally, the United States and Israel should increase cooperation on cybersecurity through a combination of military-military, public-private, and private sector collaborations. Such cooperation yields tangible benefits to both countries and serves as a force multiplier for U.S. cyber efforts. The U.S. and Israeli governments should support congressional proposals to establish a joint U.S.-Israel Cybersecurity Center of Excellence based in the United States and Israel "to leverage the experience, knowledge, and expertise of institutions of higher education, the private sector, and government entities in cyber security and protection of critical infrastructure."[62] Israel, despite its small size, now receives more than 20 percent of all global private sector investment in cyber capabilities, making it an important partner for the United States in this increasingly vital field.[63]

Renewed commitment to preserving Israel's ability to protect itself from conventional attacks and to expanding cooperation against nontraditional threats would help demonstrate—to the Israeli public and to all of Israel's adversaries—that whatever the policy differences, U.S. support for the defense of Israel is unwavering.

FOCUS ON MAKING THE IRAN NUCLEAR DEAL WORK

Another priority for the two countries should be to put aside the debate over the merits of the Iran nuclear agreement and instead focus on making it work if Iran meets the necessary requirements. Whatever anyone thought of that agreement—and President-Elect Trump has of course been harshly critical of it—the deal has now been agreed to by the

P5+1 (the five members of the UN Security Council and Germany), formally endorsed by the Security Council, and backed by nearly all major U.S. international partners, whose support for sanctions was essential to bringing Iran to the negotiating table. Although many Americans and Israelis might wish to see a "better deal," the reality is that walking away from the agreement in 2017 would isolate the United States and Israel, allow Iran a convenient excuse to resume its enrichment and plutonium production programs, and make it impossible to restore effective international sanctions. Because it is virtually inconceivable that under these circumstances Iran would make significant new concessions, the United States and Israel would likely be left with the unpalatable choice of acquiescing to a nuclear-armed Iran or using military force to set the program back for a considerably shorter time than the agreement does. In view of that reality, Americans and Israelis should make it a priority to agree on a common approach focused on how best to use the time the deal buys, always assuming that Tehran will test Washington's resolve to rigorously enforce the agreement. Israelis as security conscious as former Defense Minister Ya'alon, Chief of the General Staff Gadi Eizenkot, and former Mossad head Efraim Halevy have already started doing just that. Ya'alon is right to say that the nuclear deal is a "given" and to call on Israelis to "look to the future."[64]

The United States could do several things to help ensure Israeli buy-in if Israel is willing to try to make the agreement work. First, the United States needs to maintain the ability to deal with Iran's nuclear program militarily and make clear its willingness to do so if the situation so demands. This means not only reiterating the principle that the United States will not allow Iran to acquire a nuclear weapon, but also maintaining the military capability to fulfill that pledge. Continued upgrading of the Massive Ordnance Penetrator, the largest "bunker-busting" weapon in the U.S. arsenal, and the maintenance in the region of advanced delivery systems will be a message to Iran that though the United States wants a peaceful solution to the nuclear issue it maintains a military option if needed.[65]

Second, the United States should make clear its willingness to reimpose sanctions in the case of Iranian violations of the deal. One of the main merits of the agreement is that it maintains the U.S. ability not only to reimpose national sanctions on Iran but also to renew UN Security Council sanctions that Russia or China cannot veto. The process for reimposing such sanctions—necessary if economic pressure is to be effective—is cumbersome and requires several stages of review (by a joint commission, P5+1 foreign ministers, and an advisory board before going back to the Security Council). If the United States believes that Iran is not abiding by the agreement, however, it has the ability to put UN sanctions back in place.[66] Israel would do well to extract pledges from the United States to use this mechanism if necessary, rather than simply continue to object to its provisions.

To help quell legitimate Israeli fears of creeping Iranian noncompliance, the U.S.-Israel working group on Iran could usefully discuss what specific penalties might be imposed for specific types of violations. These steps could include delaying approvals for dual-use items (those that can be used for nonnuclear or nuclear purposes) to Iran in the "procurement channel" established by the deal, reimposing partial sanctions on Iran for partial noncompliance, or simply using the threat of renewed financial or oil sanctions, which would have an enormous deterrent effect on potential investment in Iran. The working group—which should include each country's respective intelligence agencies—would also be a good place for information-sharing about Iran's compliance with the agreement, including issues on which the reports of the International Atomic Energy Agency are lacking in specifics. These would include the size of Iran's stockpile of lightly enriched uranium, the number and type of centrifuges operating at the nuclear facility in Natanz, its heavy water supply, centrifuge research and development, and possible weaponization activities.[67] The working group would also be a good place to start planning for how best to prevent Iran's development of a nuclear weapons capability after some of the restrictions on Iran's nuclear stockpile and enrichment capability expire in 2025 or 2030—including the monitoring mechanisms that must be put in place, the maintenance of regional deterrence, and measures to prevent weaponization of any nuclear materials.

Finally, the United States could help alleviate Israeli concerns about the deal by strengthening its verification mechanisms. This would begin by ensuring that the International Atomic Energy Agency—which often faces serious staffing and budgetary shortfalls—is adequately resourced, which means not just Washington paying its dues and stepping in to fill gaps but also launching a major diplomatic effort to enhance the agency's size and budget. It also means clarifying who has responsibility for verification of all the Iran deals' provisions, some of which are ambiguous. Specifying whose responsibility it is to verify

Iran's compliance on sensitive issues such as weaponization (the deal prohibits Iran from "activities which could contribute to the design and development of a nuclear explosive device") could help quell Israeli concerns about the nuclear deal—but is only possible if the two countries are united on the objective of making it work.

All of these steps, moreover, would help reassure other countries in the region that they do not themselves need to pursue nuclear weapons programs, another important Israeli national interest.

CONTAIN IRAN'S REGIONAL DESIGNS

A coordinated U.S.-Israel approach should also include a comprehensive common agenda for addressing Iran's hegemonic designs in the region. As worried as it was over the fear that the nuclear agreement would not prevent Iran from acquiring a nuclear weapon in the long run, Israel was just as concerned that by lifting sanctions and unfreezing Iranian assets the deal would facilitate Iranian meddling in the region or even signal a possible strategic rapprochement with the United States. To reduce those concerns, the United States should admit that, at least in the short term, a more aggressive Iran is likely an unavoidable consequence of the nuclear deal and therefore should do more to demonstrate to Israel and the rest of the region that it will act vigorously to counter Iran's regional designs.

Even with the nuclear deal now in place, of course, the United States does not have diplomatic relations with Iran, does not allow its citizens and firms to invest in or—for the most part—trade with Iran, and continues to apply a long list of nonnuclear sanctions to Iran, while it bases troops in and sells billions of dollars of advanced weapons to U.S. regional partners. But it can still do more to demonstrate that it will stand by its friends in the area and not refrain from taking tough measures against Iran when they are required.

Agreement on the defense MOU, including the commitment to funding for missile defense, was a useful first step. Second, Trump should hold an early summit with leaders of the Gulf Cooperation Council, who are nearly all as concerned about Iranian meddling in the region as Israel is. Their agenda could focus not only on enhancing Gulf defensive capabilities (including missile defenses) against Iran but also on stepping up intelligence sharing and other actions to interdict

Iranian support for its proxies in Lebanon and Yemen. For now, Israeli participation in such a meeting would be a bridge too far, but a strong signal of U.S. cooperation with its Gulf partners would be reassuring to Israel as well.

Third, while fully upholding its commitments in the nuclear deal, the United States should not hesitate to penalize Iran for destabilizing actions that fall outside of that accord, including imposing sanctions for Iranian ballistic missile tests, terrorism, or human rights violations. Even the appearance that the United States is so concerned about the fate of the nuclear deal that it forgoes such measures, or takes active steps to promote rather than deter investment in Iran, only encourages Iran to leverage threats to walk away from the agreement and increases insecurity in Israel and among the United States' Arab partners in the region. Finally, the United States should continue to support Israel's right to act in its own national interest in Syria, even when that means taking military action to prevent Hezbollah from acquiring capabilities that threaten it. The United States and Israel should be open to a better relationship with a fundamentally changed Iran in the long run, unlikely as that now seems, but they need to demonstrate a joint determination to curb Iran's regional ambitions.[68]

IMPLEMENT STEPS TO IMPROVE PALESTINIAN DAILY LIFE AND PRESERVE PROSPECTS FOR NEGOTIATED PEACE

The greatest immediate challenge for the United States and Israel is the Palestinian issue, which should be a major topic for the early U.S.-Israel summit. For decades, nothing has created more tension between Jerusalem and Washington than differences over how to pursue peace, and successive U.S. presidents have acquiesced to a settlement policy by Israel that has systematically weakened prospects for comprehensive peace. No issue threatens to undermine U.S.-Israel relations—or American attitudes toward Israel—more than this one.

As noted above, many Israelis (including in the current government) argue that the centrality and urgency of the Palestinian issue is overstated, and that Israel can remain secure and prosperous without progress on it for a long time to come. Some Americans agree, pointing out that Israel has managed to thrive in recent years despite the expansion of

settlements and the absence of a peace process; Israel is expanding relations with Arab regimes, and the Palestinian issue has moved far down
on the regional diplomatic agenda (to the point that it was hardly raised
at all at the 2016 UN General Assembly).[69] But while it remains true that
Palestinian violence against Israel is currently largely contained, and that
Arab regimes will always prioritize their own security and survival over
the Palestinian issue, it is an illusion to imagine that Israel can continue to
thrive, to expand regional ties, to avoid renewed violence, and to remain
a stable, tolerant, Jewish democracy, if current trends on the West Bank
and in Gaza continue and thus end any prospect for a two-state solution.
The burgeoning strategic alignment between Israel and Arab states is
real and helpful, but the Arab world will never accept permanent Israeli
occupation of the West Bank, and no one should expect Arab governments to publicly support positions the Palestinians oppose or somehow
force them to the negotiating table. Continued Israeli settlement activity and restrictions on Palestinian development and freedom of movement remain major impediments to peace, and in the absence of a peace
agreement the continuation of current demographic trends in the West
Bank and East Jerusalem will lead to unsolvable security and political
problems for Israel, relentless criticism and international isolation, and
tensions in the U.S.-Israel relationship. The United States and Israel thus
share an interest in finding a common way forward.

Unfortunately the conditions will probably not be ripe to start negotiations on a two-state solution—the approach of U.S. administrations of
both parties for nearly twenty years—at the start of Trump's term. Even
setting aside legitimate questions about the current Israeli government's
commitment to the creation of a viable Palestinian state, comprehensive
peace negotiations with the Palestinian Authority (PA) will not likely be
fruitful until the PA resolves questions about its future—current President Mahmoud Abbas is eighty-two years old and in the twelfth year of
what was supposed to be a five-year term. Trust between Netanyahu and
Abbas is nonexistent, and even in the highly unlikely event that Abbas
were to overcome his historical reluctance to make the painful political compromises any deal would entail, it is far from clear that he would
have the legitimacy to sell it to a skeptical Palestinian population.[70] But
that does not mean that nothing can be done.

Starting at the early summit, Trump should urge Israel to take unilateral steps that would improve Palestinian lives, preserve the prospects
and improve conditions for a two-state solution, and signal a genuine

willingness to negotiate seriously on a more comprehensive agreement when those conditions permit. The list of realistic and necessary measures Israel should take is long, and would include:

- a unilateral Israeli decision to limit settlement construction to the built-up areas in the three main housing blocs it could reasonably hope to keep in land swaps negotiated with the Palestinians;

- removal of all outposts illegal under Israeli law and an end to the retroactive authorization or "legalization" of those outposts;

- budgetary allocations to provide incentives for settlers to return to Israel and an end to financial incentives for Israelis to move to settlements;

- transfer of further territory from Area C (West Bank territory under full Israeli security and administrative control) to Area B (territory under Palestinian administrative control and joint Israeli-Palestinian security control) and an expansion of Palestinian building rights in Area C;

- transfer of more territory from Area B to Area A (West Bank territory under full Palestinian security and administrative control);

- economic development initiatives and greater freedom of movement for Palestinians on the West Bank and between the West Bank and Gaza;

- minimizing incursions by Israeli security forces into Area A;

- construction of a seaport, appropriately monitored, for Gaza;

- improvement of procedures at the Allenby Bridge between the West Bank and Jordan to avoid wasteful and sometimes humiliating delays for the population;

- a commitment not to withhold Palestinian customs revenues collected on behalf of the PA by Israel; and

- a welcoming by Israel of the 2002 Arab Peace Initiative as a starting point for negotiations on comprehensive peace.

The objective of such an agenda would be to send a clear signal—to the United States, other states (including the Arab states, whose support will be critical), and, most important, the Palestinians—that Israel wants to improve daily life and dignity for Palestinians and that it is serious about coexistence with a future Palestinian state.

No one should underestimate how difficult some of these steps would be for Israel. Most have, of course, been on the agenda before, only to remain unimplemented because of the legitimate security risks and the political obstacles in their way. Palestinians, moreover, often make it difficult—both politically and for security reasons—for Israel to adopt them, through acts of terrorism and incitements to violence, and by often failing to demonstrate their commitment to peaceful coexistence with a Jewish state. Time is running out on efforts to reach peace between Israelis and Palestinians, however, and the failure to do so—especially if it results in part from Israel's refusal to take such measures—will only fuel international pressure on Israel and exacerbate the growing U.S.-Israel divisions.

If Israel agrees to take these steps, Trump should stress to the Israeli prime minister at their early summit that the United States will continue to do everything possible to protect Israel against efforts to isolate it internationally. But he should also make clear that the U.S. ability and willingness to do so will necessarily be significantly reduced—and its approach to settlements and the peace process will necessarily have to be reconsidered—if Israel chooses not to pursue the initiatives on this list. The new approach for the United States could include putting forward its own proposals for addressing the Israeli-Palestinian dispute (unilaterally, at the United Nations, or in other international groupings), supporting UN Security Council anti-settlement resolutions that are consistent with longstanding U.S. policy, and not systematically opposing or lobbying against Palestinian membership in UN or other international bodies.

REBALANCE THE PARTNERSHIP BY EXPANDING ECONOMIC COOPERATION

The core of the U.S.-Israel bilateral relationship is and will likely remain strategic cooperation, given the instability in the region and ongoing security or even existential threats to Israel. But there is also scope for a significant expansion of the economic relationship, which could not only deliver material benefits to both countries but also help compensate for some of the strategic and societal differences discussed in this report. At present, bilateral relations at the highest political level are almost exclusively focused on security issues—and usually the most contentious ones, such as the Palestinians and Iran. A joint project to enhance trade and investment ties could provide balance, highlighting for the public in both countries an aspect of the partnership that clearly benefits both sides.

Already, bilateral U.S.-Israel trade in goods and services has risen from less than $7 billion when the U.S.-Israel Free Trade Agreement was concluded in 1984 to more than $50 billion in 2016.[71] Israel is now home to more than 2,500 U.S. firms employing some 72,000 Israelis, and tens of thousands of Israelis work in the United States, often in high-skills sectors.[72] Israel is the source of nearly $9 billion in foreign direct investment (FDI) in the United States, accounting for nearly half the FDI from the entire Middle East and almost as much as China.[73] In addition, the commercial relationship is increasingly concentrated in high-tech and high-value-added areas such as chemicals, pharmaceuticals, biotech, electronics, and transportation.

To expand economic ties further, the two countries' leaders could agree to upgrade the U.S.-Israel Joint Economic Development Group, begun in the 1980s, each side appointing a senior official—reporting directly to the White House and the Prime Minister's Office—tasked with finding and exploiting areas for further cooperation. As proposed in a 2015 report by the U.S. Chamber of Commerce and the Manufacturers Association of Israel, the two sides could seek to negotiate a new trade, commerce, and innovation framework agreement that would seek to expand commercial opportunities by finding new potential for trade, addressing remaining regulatory challenges, agreeing to rules for emerging areas such as digital trade, expanding entrepreneurship, and improving the business environment by eliminating impediments in the areas of taxation, investment, and bureaucracy.[74]

One particularly promising area is energy cooperation, where American and Israeli firms (Noble Energy and Delek) are already cooperating to help Israel develop its huge offshore natural gas reserves in the Leviathan and Tamar fields. In May 2016, the Israeli High Court of Justice approved a modified deal—held up for more than a year by domestic political, legal, and regulatory challenges—that will allow development to proceed. The first gas deliveries from Leviathan are expected to come online by 2019. Development of these resources not only will help ensure Israel's domestic energy supply—and thus security—for years or decades to come but also could also turn Israel into a net gas exporter in the region. Given that potential customers include Jordan, Egypt, the Palestinian Authority, and Turkey, the issue has obvious political and geopolitical significance. The normalization of Turkey-Israel relations, which the United States pursued unsuccessfully for years following the rupture in 2009 over the Gaza flotilla incident, was finally concluded in 2016, thanks in large part to Turkey's desire for energy cooperation with Israel. The new U.S. administration should use its influence with all of Israel's potential partners to promote such ties, thus not only enhancing Israel's prosperity and security but also facilitating its political integration in the region.

Conclusion

The future of the U.S.-Israel relationship is at risk. The two countries continue to share many interests and deep cultural bonds, but the relationship is threatened by diverging strategic perspectives on a region undergoing fundamental change and by long-term demographic, political, and social trends that are undermining the pillars on which the relationship once stood. No one is well served by pretending that these risks do not exist.

For strategic, historical, and moral reasons, both governments should do all they can to reframe and revive the U.S.-Israel strategic partnership. The upcoming transition to a new U.S. administration provides an opportunity to put recent disagreements aside and to show the political will needed to reverse the negative policy trends described. This report offers several realistic and necessary steps the leaders on both sides should take as they contemplate their stewardship of this important relationship in the years to come. Although some of these steps would entail painful compromise and political risk, those leaders should understand that preserving this special relationship is worth the effort.

Endnotes

1. Israeli military and security contributions include expertise on tactical radars, robotics, airport screening techniques, armored vehicle protection, unmanned aerial systems, missile defense, and joint intelligence collection and operations against common adversaries. See Robert D. Blackwill and Walter B. Slocombe, "Israel: A Strategic Asset for the United States," Washington Institute for Near East Policy, November 2011, http://www.washingtoninstitute.org/policy-analysis/view/israel-a-strategic-asset-for-the-united-states; and Michael Eisenstadt and David Pollock, "Friends with Benefits: Why the U.S. Israeli Alliance Is Good for America," *Foreign Affairs*, November 7, 2012, http://www.washingtoninstitute.org/policy-analysis/view/friends-with-benefits-why-the-u.s.-israeli-alliance-is-good-for-america.

2. Organization for International Investment, *Foreign Direct Investment in the United States, 2016 Report*, Washington, D.C., file:///C:/Users/PHILGO~1/AppData/Local/Temp/Foreign%20Direct%20Investment%20in%20the%20United%20States%20 2016%20Report.pdf; and United States Census Bureau, *Trade in Goods with Israel, 2016*, https://www.census.gov/foreign-trade/balance/c5081.html.

3. Amos Yadlin, "Five Years Back and Five Years Forward: Israel's Strategic Environment in 2011-2015 and Policy Recommendations for 2016-2020," in *Strategic Survey for Israel 2015-2016*, eds. Shlomo Brom and Anat Kurz, 157–71 (Tel Aviv: Institute for National Security Studies, 2016), p. 165, http://www.inss.org.il/uploadImages/systemFiles/Strategic%20Survey%202015--2016_Yadlin.pdf.

4. Jeremy M. Sharp, "U.S. Foreign Aid to Israel," CRS Report no. RL33222 (Washington, DC: Congressional Research Service, June 10, 2015), p. 29; Jeremy M. Sharp, "Israel's Iron Dome Anti-Rocket System: U.S. Assistance and Coproduction," CRS Insights no. IN10158 (Washington, DC: Congressional Research Service, September 30, 2014); Missile Defence Agency, *Fiscal Year (FY) 2017 President's Budget Submission*, Department of Defense, February 2016, p. xxxi, http://comptroller.defense.gov/Portals/45/Documents/defbudget/FY2017/budget_justification/pdfs/03_RDT_and_E/MDA_RDTE_MasterJustificationBook_Missile_Defense_Agency_PB_2017_1.pdf.

5. Ross has written that "from my perspective as an original author of strategic cooperation back in the Reagan administration, I can say that the scope of the security collaboration went beyond what any previous administration had put in place." See Dennis Ross, *Doomed to Succeed: the U.S.-Israel Relationship from Truman to Obama* (New York: Farrar, Strauss and Giroux, 2015), p. 350.

6. Jeffrey Goldberg, "The Netanyahu Disaster," *The Atlantic*, January 27, 2015, http://www.theatlantic.com/international/archive/2015/01/Netanyahu-vs-Obama-on-Iran/384849/

7. "Ron Dermer: Netanyahu Speech to Congress Highlight of My DC Tenure," *Jerusalem Post*, May 11, 2016, http://www.jpost.com/Israel-News/Politics-And-Diplomacy/Ron-Dermer-Netanyahus-speech-to-Congress-is-highlight-of-my-DC-tenure-

453662; "Dermer: Israel 'Not Eager' to Battle Obama on Iran Deal, but Has No Choice," *Times of Israel*, August 15, 2015, http://www.timesofisrael.com/dermer-israel-not-eager-to-go-up-against-us-on-iran-deal-but-has-no-choice/; and Barak Ravid, "Israeli Ambassador: Netanyahu Address to Congress Worth the Price of Ties to Obama," *Haaretz*, February 17, 2015, http://www.haaretz.com/israel-news/.premium-1.642858.

8. See "Polls Show Israelis Strongly Oppose Iran Nuclear Deal," *Haaretz*, August 12, 2015, http://www.haaretz.com/israel-news/.premium-1.670835.

9. Ron Kampeas, "Israel Envoy: Nuclear Iran 'a Thousand Times' More Dangerous Than Islamic State," *Times of Israel*, September 19, 2014, http://www.timesofisrael.com/israel-envoy-nuclear-iran-a-thousand-times-more-dangerous-than-islamic-state/.

10. For a good discussion, see Michael Herzog, "Iran Still Looms Large in Israel's Threat Perception," PolicyWatch 2659, Washington Institute for Near East Policy, July 15, 2016, http://www.washingtoninstitute.org/policy-analysis/view/iran-still-looms-large-in-israels-threat-perception.

11. "Israel Bluntly Told the US Not to Cut Aid to Egypt." *Times of Israel,* October 15, 2013, http://www.timesofisrael.com/israel-bluntly-told-the-us-not-to-cut-aid-to-egypt/; and Michael Crowley, "Obama's Egypt Policy: The Israel Factor," *Time*, July 11, 2013, http://swampland.time.com/2013/07/11/obamas-egypt-policy-the-israel-factor/.

12. See Larry Hanauer, "Israel's Interests and Options in Syria," RAND, July 2016, http://www.rand.org/pubs/perspectives/PE185.html.

13. See Barak Ravid, "Netanyahu Arrives in Moscow Ahead of Putin Meet." *Haaretz.* June 6, 2016. http://www.haaretz.com/israel-news/1.723529; and Nadav Pollack, "Israeli-Russian Coordination in Syria: So Far So Good?" PolicyWatch 2529, Washington Institute for Near East Policy, December 7, 2015, http://www.washingtoninstitute.org/policy-analysis/view/israeli-russian-coordination-in-syria-so-far-so-good.

14. See joint polls by Palestinian Center for Policy and Survey Research and the Harry S. Truman Research Institute for the Advancement of Peace at the Hebrew University of Jerusalem. In another recent poll, 58.5 percent of Israelis supported a two-state solution, but that figure dropped to 46 percent when the Israelis were presented with the detailed provisions such a peace might entail. See "Palestinian-Israeli Pulse: A Joint Poll," Palestinian Center for Policy and Survey Research, The Israel Democracy Institute, Konrad Adenauer Stiftung, EU Peacebuilding Initiative, August 22, 2016, http://www.pcpsr.org/en/node/662.

15. "Israel's Religiously Divided Society," Pew Research Center, March 8, 2016, http://www.pewforum.org/2016/03/08/israels-religiously-divided-society/; "The Peace Index – June 2016," Israel Institute for Democracy, June 2016, http://www.peaceindex.org/files/Peace_Index_Data_June_2016-Eng.pdf.

16. "Report of the Middle East Quartet," Foundation for Middle East Peace, July 2016, p. 4, http://fmep.org/resource/report-middle-east-quartet/.

17. See Chaim Levinson, "Is Netanyahu Responsible for Rise in Settler Numbers?" *Haaretz,* October 14, 2015, http://www.haaretz.com/israel-news/.premium-1.680304; "Netanyahu and the Settlements," *New York Times*, March 12, 2015, http://www.nytimes.com/interactive/2015/03/12/world/middleeast/netanyahu-west-bank-settlements-israel-election.html?_r=0; Diaa Hadid, "U.S. Rebukes Israel Over New Settlement Activity in East Jerusalem," *New York Times*, July 29, 2016, http://www.nytimes.com/2016/07/29/world/middleeast/israel-east-jerusalem.html. The Quartet report notes that though the issuance of new settlement plans and tenders have slowed markedly since 2014, the rate of construction starts during this period has remained consistent, as previously approved plans and tenders allow building to continue even in the absence of new approvals. "Report of the Middle East Quartet," p. 4.

18. Isabel Kershner, "Israel Quietly Legalizes Pirate Outposts in the West Bank," *New York Times*, August 30, 2016, http://www.nytimes.com/2016/08/31/world/middleeast/israel-west-bank-outposts-mitzpe-danny.html.

19. "Report of the Middle East Quartet," p. 5.

20. "Netanyahu Rejects U.S. Criticism of Settlement Expansion as 'Unacceptable,'" *Haaretz*, July 6, 2016, http://www.haaretz.com/israel-news/1.729385; and Isabel Kershner, "Israel Approves Additional Funding for Settlements in West Bank," *New York Times*, June 19, 2016, http://www.nytimes.com/2016/06/20/world/middleeast/israel-west-bank-settlements-palestinians.html?_r=0.

21. See Barak Ravid, "Netanyahu Tells Knesset Panel, We Have Defeated the BDS Movement," *Haaretz*, July 25, 2016, http://www.haaretz.com/israel-news/1.733113.

22. See Netanyahu's interview with Jeffrey Goldberg, "Netanyahu Says Obama Got Syria Right," *Bloomberg View*, May 22, 2014, http://www.bloomberg.com/view/articles/2014-05-22/netanyahu-says-obama-got-syria-right.

23. The State Department said Netanyahu's remarks were "inappropriate and unhelpful," and many critics rejected Netanyahu's comparison between Israeli Arabs who have lived in Israel for generations and are Israeli citizens and the settlers who have moved into disputed territory occupied after war and are Israeli, and not Palestinian citizens. Isabel Kershner, "Benjamin Netanyahu Draws Fire After Saying Palestinians Support Ethnic Cleansing," *New York Times*, September 12, 2016, http://www.nytimes.com/2016/09/13/world/middleeast/benjamin-netanyahu-ethnic-cleansing.html

24. The quote is from liberal Israeli editor Benny Ziffer, cited by conservative Israeli scholar Martin Kramer in Martin Kramer, "Israel and the Post-American Middle East: Why the Status Quo Is Sustainable," *Foreign Affairs*, June 8, 2016, http://www.foreignaffairs.com/articles/united-states/2016-06-08/israel-and-post-american-middle-east.

25. Ya'alon, "Kerry Should Win His Nobel and Leave Us Alone," *Ynet.com*, January 14, 2014, http://www.ynetnews.com/articles/0,7340,L-4476582,00.html.

26. Jodi Rudoren, "Netanyahu Says No to Statehood for Palestinians," *New York Times*, March 16, 2015, http://www.nytimes.com/2015/03/17/world/middleeast/benjamin-netanyahu-campaign-settlement.html.

27. The White House, "White House Chief of Staff Denis McDonough Remarks as Prepared at J Street Annual Conference," Press Release, March 25, 2013, http://www.whitehouse.gov/the-press-office/2015/03/23/white-house-chief-staff-denis-mcdonough-remarks-prepared-j-street-annual.

28. John Kerry, "Brookings Institution's 2015 Saban Forum Keynote Address," December 5, 2015, http://www.state.gov/secretary/remarks/2015/12/250388.htm.

29. Peter Beaumont, "US Feels 'Overwhelming Frustration' With Israeli Government, Says Biden," *Guardian*, April 19, 2016, http://www.theguardian.com/us-news/2016/apr/19/joe-biden-us-overwhelming-frustration-israeli-government.

30. See Nathan Thrall, "Obama and Palestine: The Last Chance," *New York Review of Books*, September 10, 2016, http://www.nybooks.com/daily/2016/09/10/obama-israel-palestine-parameters-resolution-the-last-chance/.

31. Tal Shalev, "Netanyahu in Message to White House: Don't Present US Proposal for Solution of Conflict," *Walla!*, August 29, 2016; and Patricia Zengerle and Jeffrey Heller, "Netanyahu Hopes U.S. Will Reject U.N. Resolution on Palestinian Statehood," Reuters, March 22, 2016.

32. See Sarah Dutton, Jennifer De Pinto, Anthony Salvanto, and Fred Backus, "How Do Americans View Israel?" CBS News, March 3, 2015 http:/www.cbsnews.com/news/how-do-americans-view-israel/; and Margaret Talev, "Bloomberg Politics National Poll Finds Deep Partisan Split on Israel and Iran," Bloomberg Politics, April 15, 2015, http://www.bloomberg.com/politics/articles/2015-04-15/bloomberg-politics-national-poll-finds-deep-partisan-split-on-israel-and-iran.

33. Lydia Saad, "American's Views Toward Israel Remain Firmly Positive," Gallup, February 29, 2016, http://www.gallup.com/poll/189626/americans-views-toward-israel-remain-firmly-positive.aspx; and Bob Burnett, "Vote No on Armageddon," *Huffington Post*, June 30, 2015, http://www.huffingtonpost.com/bob-burnett/vote-no-on-armageddon_b_7179908.html.

34. "Israel's Religiously Divided Society."

35. See Yinan Cohen and Neve Gordon, "The Demographic Success of the West Bank Settlement," Columbia University, December 2012, http://www.columbia.edu/~yc2444/pages/Demographic%20Success%20of%20the%20West%20Bank%20Settlers.html; Neri Zilber, "Israel's Internal Demographic Disaster," *National Interest* http://www.columbia.edu/~yc2444/pages/Demographic%20Success%20of%20West%20Bank%20Settlers.html; and "Statistics on Settlements and Settler Population," B'Tselem, May 11, 2015, http://www.btselem.org/settlements/statistics.

36. Lieberman's explanation for his view was that Israelis faced security risks and had to decide themselves how to deal with them whether Americans—or American Jews— agreed with them. See Thomas L. Friedman, "The Many Mideast Solutions," *New York Times*, February 10, 2016, http://www.nytimes.com/2016/02/10/opinion/the-many-mideast-solutions.html; and Chemi Shalev, "Widening Rift Between American Jews and Israel on Painful Display at Saban Forum," *Forward*, December 6, 2015, http://forward.com/opinion/326188/widening-rift-between-american-jews-and-israel-on-painful-display-at-saban/.

37. According to 2014 Pew polls, 46 percent of Israeli Jews now see themselves first as Jewish, compared with 35 percent who see themselves first as Israeli. The same polls showed a plurality of Israeli Jews (49 percent to 45) agreed with the proposition that "Arabs should be expelled or transferred from Israel." See "Israel's Religiously Divided Society." See also polls of young Israelis taken by the Friedrich Ebert Foundation in 2011, which also showed majority preference for a "strong leader" over the "rule of law." Cited in Or Kashti, "Poll: Younger Israelis Moving Much Farther to the Right Politically," *Haaretz*, March 31, 2011, http://www.haaretz.com/poll-young-israelis-moving-much-farther-to-the-right-politically-1.353187.

38. Dana H. Allin and Steven Simon, *Our Separate Ways: The Struggle for the Future of the U.S.-Israel Alliance* (New York: Public Affairs, 2016), p. x.

39. In 2006, for Americans born after 1980 the gap in favor of Israelis was 42 points. "Views of Israel and Palestinians," Pew Research Center, May 5, 2016, http://www.people-press.org/2016/05/05/5-views-of-israel-and-palestinians/.

40. Shibley Telhami and Katayoun Kishi, "Widening Democratic Party Divisions on the Israeli-Palestinian Issue," *Washington Post*, December 15, 2014, http://www.washingtonpost.com/blogs/monkey-cage/wp/2014/12/15/widening-democratic-party-divisions-on-the-israeli-palestinian-issue/.

41. "Connection With and Attitudes Toward Israel," Pew Research Center, October 1, 2013, www.pewforum.org/2013/10/10chapter5-connection-with-and-attitudes-towards-israel/, cited in Ross, *Doomed to Succeed*, p. 406.

42. Cited in Dov Waxman, *Trouble in the Tribe: The American Jewish Conflict Over Israel* (Princeton, NJ: Princeton University Press, 2016), p. 50.

43. "Sanctions Against Israel: A Campaign That Is Gathering Weight," *Economist*, February 8, 2014, http://www.economist.com/news/middle-east-and-africa/21595948-israels-politicians-sound-rattled-campaign-isolate-their-country. For a list of universities with BDS referendums in 2014 and 2015, see "BDS on American College Campuses: 2014-15 Year-in-Review," Anti-Defamation League, http://www.adl.org/israel-international/anti-israel-activity/c/bds-on-american-college-2014-2015.html#.V2sKHvkrKUl.

44. Eric Levitz, "Bernie Sanders Will Press Democrats to Pursue More 'Even-Handed' Approach to Israel-Palestine Conflict," *New York Magazine*, http://nymag.com/daily/intelligencer/2016/05/bernie-sanderss-surprising-platform-priority.html.

45. See Jason Horowitz and Maggie Haberman, "A Split Over Israel Threatens the Democrats' Hopes for Unity," *New York Times*, June 14, 2016, http://www.nytimes.com/2016/05/26/us/politics/bernie-sanders-israel-democratic-convention.html; Shmuel Rosner, "Israel's Problem with the Democratic Party," *New York Times*, June 9, 2016, http://www.nytimes.com/2016/06/10/opinion/israels-problem-with-the-democratic-party.html.

46. Telhami and Kishi, "Widening Democratic Party Divisions."

47. Ibid.

48. See Jens Manuel Krogstad, "2016 Electorate Will Be the Most Diverse in U.S. History," Pew Research Center, February 3, 2016, http://www.pewresearch.org/fact-tank/2016/02/03/2016-electorate-will-be-the-most-diverse-in-u-s-history/.

49. Paul Taylor, "The Next America," Pew Research Survey, http://www.pewresearch.org/next-america/.

50. See Waxman, *Trouble in the Tribe*, p. 214.

51. Shibley Telhami, "American Attitudes Toward the Middle East and Israel," Brookings Institution, December 4, 2015, http://www.brookings.edu/wp-content/uploads/2016/07/2015-Poll-Key-Findings-Final-1.pdf.

52. Samantha Smith and Carroll Doherty, "5 Facts About How Americans View the Israeli-Palestinian Conflict," Pew Research Center, May 23, 2016, http://www.pewresearch.org/fact-tank/2016/05/23/5-facts-about-how-americans-view-the-israeli-palestinian-conflict/.

53. Telhami and Kishi, "Widening Democratic Party Divisions."

54. Gregg Carlstrom, "Why Israel Loves Donald Trump," *Politico*, March 20, 2016, http://www.politico.com/magazine/story/2016/03/donald-trump-israel-2016-netanyahu-213748.

55. See Jacob Kornbluh, "In About-Face for U.S. Foreign Policy, GOP to Drop Support for Two-State Solution," *Jewish Insider*, July 11, 2016, http://www.haaretz.com/israel-news/1.730322.

56. See Armin Rosen, "How the Republican and Democratic Platforms Differ on Israel," *Tablet*, July 14, 2016, http://www.tabletmag.com/scroll/208036/how-the-republican-and-democratic-platforms-differ-on-israel.

57. "Wide Partisan Divide Over Iran Deal," Pew Research Center, July 21, 2015, http://www.people-press.org/2015/07/21/iran-nuclear-agreement-meets-with-public-skepticism/7-21-2015_iran_02/.

58. "The Complete Transcript of Netanyahu's Speech to Congress," *Washington Post*, March 3, 2015.

59. See Michael Herzog, "Iran Still Looms Large in Israel's Threat Perception," PolicyWatch 2659, Washington Institute for Near East Policy, July 15, 2016, http://www.washingtoninstitute.org/policy-analysis/view/iran-still-looms-large-in-israels-threat-perception.

60. The White House, "Fact Sheet: Memorandum of Understanding Reached with Israel," Press Release, September 14, 2016, https://www.whitehouse.gov/the-press-office/2016/09/14/fact-sheet-memorandum-understanding-reached-israel.

61. Amos Harel, "Israel's Evolving Military," *Foreign Affairs* 95, no. 4 (July/August 2016): 44; Josie Ensor, "What Is in Hamas's New Deadly Arsenal?" *Telegraph*, July 9, 2014, http://www.telegraph.co.uk/news/worldnews/middleeast/palestinianauthority/10955514/What-is-in-Hamass-new-deadly-arsenal.html.

62. Rep. David N. Cicilline [D-RI-1], H.R. 4860, United States - Israel Cybersecurity Cooperation Act, 114th Congress, March 23, 2016, http://www.congress.gov/bill/114th-congress/house-bill/4860.

63. See John Reed, "Israel Cyber-Security Lures Growing Share of Investment," *Financial Times*, January 12, 2016, http://www.ft.com/cms/s/0/dfa5c916-b90e-11e5-b151-8e15c9a029fb.html#axzz4JbPoS0Vb.

64. See "Ya'alon: Nuclear Deal Dispute Between Israel, U.S. Is Over," *Haaretz*, October 29, 2015; Graham Allison, "Is Iran Still Israel's Top Threat?" *Atlantic*, March 8, 2016.

65. See Julian E. Barnes and Adam Entous, "Pentagon Upgraded Biggest 'Bunker Buster' Bomb as Iran Talks Unfolded," *Wall Street Journal*, April 3, 2015, http://www.wsj.com/articles/pentagon-worked-to-improve-biggest-bunker-buster-bomb-as-iran-talks-unfolded-1428078456.

66. If the issue of alleged Iranian noncompliance is unresolved after completion of this review process, the issue is referred back to the Security Council, where a positive vote is required to continue sanctions lifting. If the veto-wielding United States refused to vote in favor, the sanctions in the old UN Security Council resolutions would be restored. See *Joint Comprehensive Plan of Action*, Vienna, July 14, 2015, paras. 36-37, http://www.state.gov/e/eb/tfs/spi/iran/jcpoa/.

67. See David Albright, Serena Kelleher-Vergantini, and Andrea Stricker, "IAEA's Second JCPOA Report: Key Information Still Missing," Institute for Science and International Security, http://isis-online.org/uploads/isis-reports/documents/Second_JCPOA_Post-Implementation_Day_Report_May_31_2016_Final.pdf.

68. See Philip Gordon, "The Long View: Will the Nuclear Deal Transform Iran?" *American Interest*, May 3, 2016, http://www.the-american-interest.com/2016/05/03/will-the-nuclear-deal-transform-iran/.

69. See Walter Russell Mead, "The Real Middle East Story," *The American Interest*, September 23, 2016.

70. According to the recent joint survey cited, although a small majority of Palestinians (51 percent) still supports a two-state solution, only 39 percent support a permanent agreement package that would include realistic Palestinian concessions on permanent status issues (including a demilitarized Palestinian state; Israeli withdrawal to Green Line with equal territorial exchange, family unification in Israel of one hundred thousand Palestinian refugees, West Jerusalem as the capital of Israel, and East Jerusalem as the capital of Palestine; respective sovereignty in different parts of Jerusalem; and the end of conflict and claims). See "Palestinian-Israeli Pulse."

71. See U.S. Census Bureau figures, http://www.census.gov/foreign-trade/balance/c5081.html; and "June 15, 2016: Ambassador Daniel B. Shapiro's Remarks at the 2016 Herzliya Conference," U.S. Embassy in Israel, http://il.usembassy.gov/june-15-2016-ambassador-daniel-b-shapiros-remarks-2016-herzliya-conference/.

72. "June 15, 2016"; and "Israelis Are Among the Top Recipients of U.S. Highly Skilled Work Visas Israeli Commercial Mission," http://itrade.gov.il/us-dc/2013/08/13/israelis-are-among-the-top-recipients-of-u-s-highly-skilled-work-visas/.

73. For data until 2014, see Organization for International Investment, "Foreign Direct Investment in the United States, 2016 Report," http://ofii.org/sites/default/files/Foreign%20Direct%20Investment%20in%20the%20United%20States%202016%20Report.pdf.

74. For this and other useful suggestions, see U.S. Chamber of Commerce and Manufacturers Association of Israel, "Re-energizing the U.S.-Israel Economic and Commercial Relationship: A Policy Framework for Trade, Investment, and Innovation," December 2015, http://www.uschamber.com/sites/default/files/documents/files/2015_re-0energizing_the_u.s.-israel_commercial_relationship.pdf.

About the Authors

Robert D. Blackwill is a former deputy assistant to the president, deputy national security advisor for strategic planning, and presidential envoy to Iraq under George W. Bush. He was U.S. Ambassador to India from 2001 to 2003. He is the coauthor of *War By Other Means: Geoeconomics and Statecraft, Xi Jinping on the Global Stage, Revising U.S. Grand Strategy Toward China, Lee Kuan Yew: The Grand Master's Insights on China, the United States, and the World*, and editor of *Iran: The Nuclear Challenge*. Currently, he is the Henry A. Kissinger senior fellow for U.S. foreign policy at the Council on Foreign Relations.

Philip H. Gordon is a senior fellow at the Council on Foreign Relations. He served as special assistant to the president and White House coordinator for the Middle East, North Africa, and the Gulf region from 2013 to 2015 and as assistant secretary of state for European and Eurasian affairs from 2009 to 2013. He has a PhD from Johns Hopkins University's School of Advanced International Studies and has published numerous books and articles about U.S. foreign policy, the Middle East, and international security. Gordon writes regularly for publications such as *Foreign Affairs*, the *Washington Post*, *Financial Times*, and *Politico*.

Council Special Reports

Published by the Council on Foreign Relations

Securing a Democratic Future for Myanmar
Priscilla A. Clapp; CSR No. 75, March 2016
A Center for Preventive Action Report

Xi Jinping on the Global Stage: Chinese Foreign Policy Under a Powerful but Exposed Leader
Robert D. Blackwill and Kurt M. Campbell; CSR No. 74, February 2016
An International Institutions and Global Governance Program Report

Enhancing U.S. Support for Peace Operations in Africa
Paul D. Williams; CSR No. 73, May 2015

Revising U.S. Grand Strategy Toward China
Robert D. Blackwill and Ashley J. Tellis; CSR No. 72, March 2015
An International Institutions and Global Governance Program Report

Strategic Stability in the Second Nuclear Age
Gregory D. Koblentz; CSR No. 71, November 2014

U.S. Policy to Counter Nigeria's Boko Haram
John Campbell; CSR No. 70, November 2014
A Center for Preventive Action Report

Limiting Armed Drone Proliferation
Micah Zenko and Sarah Kreps; CSR No. 69, June 2014
A Center for Preventive Action Report

Reorienting U.S. Pakistan Strategy: From Af-Pak to Asia
Daniel S. Markey; CSR No. 68, January 2014

Afghanistan After the Drawdown
Seth G. Jones and Keith Crane; CSR No. 67, November 2013
A Center for Preventive Action Report

The Future of U.S. Special Operations Forces
Linda Robinson; CSR No. 66, April 2013

Reforming U.S. Drone Strike Policies
Micah Zenko; CSR No. 65, January 2013
A Center for Preventive Action Report

The United States in the New Asia
Evan A. Feigenbaum and Robert A. Manning; CSR No. 50, November 2009
An International Institutions and Global Governance Program Report

Intervention to Stop Genocide and Mass Atrocities: International Norms and U.S. Policy
Matthew C. Waxman; CSR No. 49, October 2009
An International Institutions and Global Governance Program Report

Enhancing U.S. Preventive Action
Paul B. Stares and Micah Zenko; CSR No. 48, October 2009
A Center for Preventive Action Report

The Canadian Oil Sands: Energy Security vs. Climate Change
Michael A. Levi; CSR No. 47, May 2009
A Maurice R. Greenberg Center for Geoeconomic Studies Report

The National Interest and the Law of the Sea
Scott G. Borgerson; CSR No. 46, May 2009

Lessons of the Financial Crisis
Benn Steil; CSR No. 45, March 2009
A Maurice R. Greenberg Center for Geoeconomic Studies Report

Global Imbalances and the Financial Crisis
Steven Dunaway; CSR No. 44, March 2009
A Maurice R. Greenberg Center for Geoeconomic Studies Report

Eurasian Energy Security
Jeffrey Mankoff; CSR No. 43, February 2009

Preparing for Sudden Change in North Korea
Paul B. Stares and Joel S. Wit; CSR No. 42, January 2009
A Center for Preventive Action Report

Averting Crisis in Ukraine
Steven Pifer; CSR No. 41, January 2009
A Center for Preventive Action Report

Congo: Securing Peace, Sustaining Progress
Anthony W. Gambino; CSR No. 40, October 2008
A Center for Preventive Action Report

Deterring State Sponsorship of Nuclear Terrorism
Michael A. Levi; CSR No. 39, September 2008

China, Space Weapons, and U.S. Security
Bruce W. MacDonald; CSR No. 38, September 2008

Sovereign Wealth and Sovereign Power: The Strategic Consequences of American Indebtedness
Brad W. Setser; CSR No. 37, September 2008
A Maurice R. Greenberg Center for Geoeconomic Studies Report

Securing Pakistan's Tribal Belt
Daniel S. Markey; CSR No. 36, July 2008 (web-only release) and August 2008
A Center for Preventive Action Report

Avoiding Transfers to Torture
Ashley S. Deeks; CSR No. 35, June 2008

Global FDI Policy: Correcting a Protectionist Drift
David M. Marchick and Matthew J. Slaughter; CSR No. 34, June 2008
A Maurice R. Greenberg Center for Geoeconomic Studies Report

Dealing with Damascus: Seeking a Greater Return on U.S.-Syria Relations
Mona Yacoubian and Scott Lasensky; CSR No. 33, June 2008
A Center for Preventive Action Report

Climate Change and National Security: An Agenda for Action
Joshua W. Busby; CSR No. 32, November 2007
A Maurice R. Greenberg Center for Geoeconomic Studies Report

Planning for Post-Mugabe Zimbabwe
Michelle D. Gavin; CSR No. 31, October 2007
A Center for Preventive Action Report

The Case for Wage Insurance
Robert J. LaLonde; CSR No. 30, September 2007
A Maurice R. Greenberg Center for Geoeconomic Studies Report

Reform of the International Monetary Fund
Peter B. Kenen; CSR No. 29, May 2007
A Maurice R. Greenberg Center for Geoeconomic Studies Report

Nuclear Energy: Balancing Benefits and Risks
Charles D. Ferguson; CSR No. 28, April 2007

Nigeria: Elections and Continuing Challenges
Robert I. Rotberg; CSR No. 27, April 2007
A Center for Preventive Action Report

The Economic Logic of Illegal Immigration
Gordon H. Hanson; CSR No. 26, April 2007
A Maurice R. Greenberg Center for Geoeconomic Studies Report

The United States and the WTO Dispute Settlement System
Robert Z. Lawrence; CSR No. 25, March 2007
A Maurice R. Greenberg Center for Geoeconomic Studies Report

Bolivia on the Brink
Eduardo A. Gamarra; CSR No. 24, February 2007
A Center for Preventive Action Report

After the Surge: The Case for U.S. Military Disengagement From Iraq
Steven N. Simon; CSR No. 23, February 2007

A New Beginning: Strategies for a More Fruitful Dialogue with the Muslim World
Craig Charney and Nicole Yakatan; CSR No. 7, May 2005

Power-Sharing in Iraq
David L. Phillips; CSR No. 6, April 2005
A Center for Preventive Action Report

*Giving Meaning to "Never Again": Seeking an Effective Response to the Crisis
in Darfur and Beyond*
Cheryl O. Igiri and Princeton N. Lyman; CSR No. 5, September 2004

Freedom, Prosperity, and Security: The G8 Partnership with Africa: Sea Island 2004 and Beyond
J. Brian Atwood, Robert S. Browne, and Princeton N. Lyman; CSR No. 4, May 2004

Addressing the HIV/AIDS Pandemic: A U.S. Global AIDS Strategy for the Long Term
Daniel M. Fox and Princeton N. Lyman; CSR No. 3, May 2004
Cosponsored with the Milbank Memorial Fund

Challenges for a Post-Election Philippines
Catharin E. Dalpino; CSR No. 2, May 2004
A Center for Preventive Action Report

Stability, Security, and Sovereignty in the Republic of Georgia
David L. Phillips; CSR No. 1, January 2004
A Center for Preventive Action Report

Note: Council Special Reports are available for download from CFR's website, www.cfr.org.
For more information, email publications@cfr.org.

www.ingramcontent.com/pod-product-compliance
Lightning Source LLC
Chambersburg PA
CBHW060522280326
41933CB00014B/3072